The snow house

Written by Keith Gaines

Illustrated by Margaret de Souza

Nelson

"Can Rob play in the snow?"
said Kim.

"Yes,"
said Mum.
"You and Rob and the dog
can make a snowman."

Rob and Kim made a snowman.
Rob put a cap
on the snowman's head.

Rob threw a snowball at Kim,
but it hit the dog's head.

Kim threw a snowball at Rob.

"Let's make a house
for the snowman,"
said Kim.
"Let's make a snow house."

"A house is made of bricks," said Rob.

"How can we make snow bricks?"

Kim got a box.
She put lots of snow in the box.

Then she jumped up and down on the box.

The snow fell out of the box.

Kim made the snow bricks and Rob made the snow house.

"Don't forget the roof,"
said Rob.
"We can make a roof
with a big bit of wood."

Rob and Kim
got a big bit of wood.
They put the wood
on the snow house.

"We can put snow on the roof," said Kim.

"Oh, no,"
said Kim.
"It is too small for the snowman."

"There is no room for him . . .
but there is for us."